Discovering Cities

Birmingham

Zinc Bar, canal basin.
Photo: Peter J. Larkham

Great Western Arcade.
Photo: Peter J. Larkham

The Town Hall and Iron Man.
Photo: Peter J. Larkham

New Street/Corporation Street.
Photo: Peter J. Larkham

Argent Centre.
Photo: Peter J. Larkham

View to Council House.
Photo: Peter J. Larkham

Gas Street.
Photo: Peter J. Larkham

Bournville village green.
Photo: Peter J. Larkham

Discovering Cities

Birmingham

Peter J. Larkham
University of Central England,
Birmingham

Series Editors
Peter S. Fox and
Christopher M. Law

Geographical
Association

Preface

© Peter J. Larkham

BRINDLEYPLACE

The variety and complexity of cities as revealed in their built form has been a source of fascination to the local resident and visitor alike. Can a clear spatial structure be discerned? Why do activities cluster in distinctive quarters or zones? How do relict features throw light on the constantly evolving city?

For a long time, human geographers, regional economists, urban sociologists and local historians have sought to understand the processes which shape the city. The growth (or decline) of the city is affected by local, regional and global economic forces. The forces which shape the internal structure of the city are many and varied. There is a market in land that influences the pattern of land use and change. Public policies are often significant but can be complex to understand and difficult to follow. Social factors such as those of class and ethnic community identities are also important.

Written by urban geographers with vast knowledge and experience of the city in question, *Discovering Cities* gathers these issues together in concise and practical guides, illustrated with colour maps and photographs, to enable an enhanced perspective of cities of the British Isles.

Peter S. Fox, Chilwell Comprehensive School, Chilwell, Nottingham

Christopher M. Law, Visiting Fellow, University of Salford and Research Associate, University of Gloucestershire

Acknowledgements

Some of this text is based on work undertaken for the *Encyclopedia of Urban Cultures* (Ember and Ember, 2002) and for the Centre for Contemporary Culture, Barcelona. I am grateful to Terry Slater
for commenting on an early draft.

ISBN 1 84377 035 0
First published 2003
Impression number 10 9 8 7 6 5 4 3 2 1
Year 2005 2004 2003

Published by the Geographical Association, 160 Solly Street, Sheffield S1 4BF.
Website: www.geography.org.uk
E-mail: ga@geography.org.uk

The Geographical Association is a registered charity: no 313129.

The Publications Officer of the GA would be happy to hear from other potential authors who have ideas for geography books. You may contact the Officer via the GA at the address above. The views expressed in this publication are those of the author and do not necessarily represent those of the Geographical Association.

Editing: Rose Pipes
Design and typesetting: Arkima, Leeds
Cartography: Paul Coles
Printing and binding: EspaceGrafic, Spain

Contents

© Peter J. Larkham

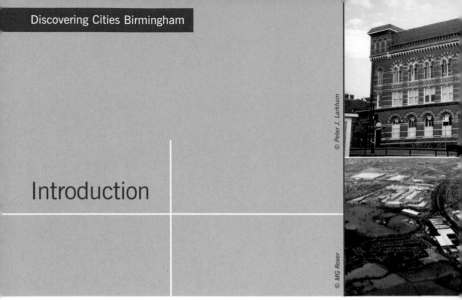

© Peter J. Larkham

© MG Rover

Introduction

Birmingham has long been seen as England's 'second city', the major provincial capital and product of the Industrial Revolution. It is now a business, administrative and cultural centre and forms the largest all-purpose municipal administrative unit in Europe.

On a visit to the city in 1885, the Czech composer Antonin Dvorak (1841-1904) said: 'I'm here in this immense industrial city where they make excellent knives, scissors, springs, files and goodness knows what else, and, besides these, music too. And how well! It's terrifying how much the people here manage to achieve'.

Nearly one hundred years later the architectural historian Sir Nikolaus Pevsner noted that 'The astonishing growth of Birmingham into the second largest city in the kingdom immediately raises the fascinating question of why and how this has come about. There seems to be no obvious and completely satisfying answer!' (Pevsner and Wedgewood, 1966).

Part of the answer to Pevsner's observation is that Birmingham has always been a city founded on trade: it was once described as 'the city of a thousand trades'. It grew as a market because it was located on or near to sources of raw materials. It became world-famous for supplying finished products, from shoe buckles to guns, jewellery and, in the twentieth century, cars. It now hosts many business services and has a profile based on business tourism, cultural facilities and related events.

Part of the answer also lies in innovation. For example, it was in Birmingham that the 'Spinning Jenny', cotton wool, oxygen, electro-plating and the pneumatic tyre were first used or invented. In addition, Boulton and Watt patented the steam engine here, the first medical X-ray was taken here in 1896, and pioneering development work on radar was undertaken in the city during the Second World War. Recent studies have confirmed that the majority of English patentable inventions originated within some 50km of the city, and about 25% of British exports come from Birmingham.

Although Birmingham, in common with most industrial cities, has suffered from pollution and congestion, and more recently the problems of cuts and closures in its major industrial employers, a concerted programme of promotion, inward investment and redevelopment has sought to re-present the city as a thriving international business and cultural centre.

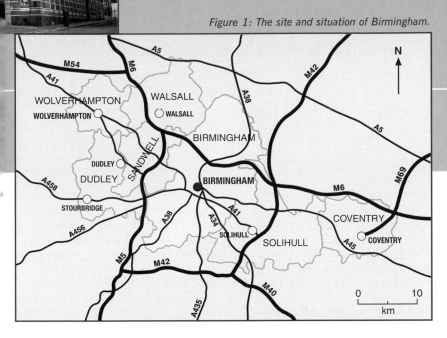

Figure 1: The site and situation of Birmingham.

Site and situation

The City of Birmingham is a large, local government metropolitan district at the heart of the West Midlands metropolitan county (Figure 1). The city is located at 52° 30'N and 1° 50'W, a few kilometres north of the country's geographical centre and immediately south-east of the historic industrial conurbation known as the Black Country.

To the south-east is Solihull, originally a small medieval market town and now largely a dormitory suburb and shopping centre. Further south-east, separated from Birmingham by a section of Green Belt but still within the county, is the city of Coventry. The industrial Black Country comprises the metropolitan boroughs of Dudley, Sandwell and Walsall, and Wolverhampton (given city status to mark the millennium).

At the 2001 Census Birmingham's total population was 977,091. At the 1991 Census, the ethnic breakdown was 78.5% white, 5.9% black, 13.5% Indian, Pakistani and Bangladeshi, and 2.1% Chinese and other Asian. Other research suggests that just under 20% of the 'whites' are Irish. The result is great social and cultural diversity. The city's catchment area is well-served by road and rail networks and extends for about 80km in all directions from the city centre. Six million people live within this area, many of whom commute to work in the city and/or make regular visits to its various facilities.

Birmingham is a major node within the national rail network, a link-point within the trans-national corridor which connects Scotland and Ireland via the Channel Tunnel to mainland Europe. New Street is one of Europe's busiest stations in terms of train movements, and is on the West Coast Main Line link between London (Euston) and Scotland (Glasgow and Inverness). There is also a slower

Table 1: Growth in population and area.
Source: Census returns.

Year	Area (ha)	Population
1801	3400	70,600
1851	3400	232,000
1901	5100	522,000
1951	20,600	1,112,600
2001	26,400	977,091

alternative rail link from Birmingham Moor Street station to London (Marylebone). The Midland Metro is a light rail system which links Birmingham, through the Black Country, to Wolverhampton. This first line opened in May 1999 at a cost of £45 million. A £55.5 million extension scheduled for 2003-05 will run through Birmingham city centre, and additional routes are proposed.

As well as being served by Birmingham International airport, the city is well-connected by road, being at the hub of the motorway network (with the M5 to the south-west, M6 north-west, M6/M1 and M40 south, and M42 and M69 east to west). A new toll motorway is under construction around the north-east of the conurbation. This has been designed to relieve congestion, as the M5/M6 section through the conurbation (including 'Spaghetti Junction', one of Europe's largest motorway junctions) is the country's most congested stretch of motorway. A western bypass is still under discussion, as it has been since 1945! Birmingham itself has a network of inner, middle and outer ring roads, the inner of which has come to be regarded as a 'concrete collar' restricting the further development of the CBD. Work is currently under way to downgrade it.

The large-scale development of Birmingham began at the start of the eighteenth century, powered by industrialised production methods, new routes and forms of transport and large-scale trade. Growth continued at an increasing pace over the next 150 years (Table 1). Owing to periodic changes in administrative boundaries, it is difficult to compare one year with another (for 1800 and 1851 particularly) in terms of the city's area and population, but what is quite clear is that the pace and scale of change increased significantly in the early years of the twentieth century.

The city's rapid growth, its reliance on heavy industrial production and changes in the ethnic and socio-economic characteristics of its population meant that by the late twentieth century the city faced a number of problems and challenges, including physical dereliction, high unemployment, pollution and congestion. In response, the city implemented a range of planning and development policies, as well as programmes of promotion, inward investment and regeneration. The result of this re-presentation of the city is that it is now a thriving international business and cultural centre. This make-over has been so successful that the city was recently ranked by the *Rough Guide* as a more desirable place of residence than Rome, Milan or Barcelona! (Johnson, 2002).

© Peter J. Larkham

Historical geography

er J. Larkham

Contents

Westley, 1731

© Field Archaeology Unit, University of Birmingham

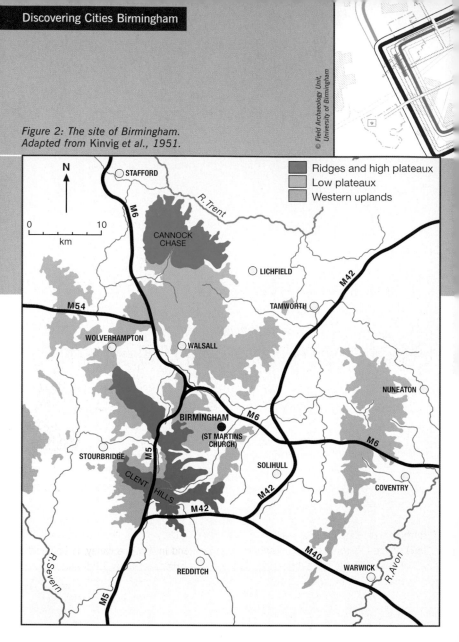

Figure 2: The site of Birmingham.
Adapted from Kinvig et al., 1951.

© Field Archaeology Unit, University of Birmingham

Legend:
- Ridges and high plateaux
- Low plateaux
- Western uplands

Pre-industrial settlement and early growth

Birmingham is in the centre of an upland plateau that has been isolated by the valleys of the Rivers Trent, Severn and Avon and their tributaries (Figure 2). The plateau is almost bisected by the River Tame, and the core of the city lies by the River Rea, a tributary of the Tame. The plateau is largely sandstone, while the main rock in the river valleys and the area south and east of the city centre is Mercian mudstone. Between the city centre and the Black Country

coalfield is a broad expanse of glacial clay. Soils here are poorly-drained and heavy and support a belt of barren heath, frequently used as a common.

The only evidence of Roman settlement in the area is a military camp at Metchley (SW of the city centre, by the Queen Elizabeth hospital) on the Roman road known as Ryknild Street. Part of this road survives in Sutton and it joins Watling Street (now the A5) at Letocetum (Wall), near Lichfield. In the Anglo-Saxon period Tamworth (to the NE) was a far more significant settlement than Birmingham.

THE "OLD CROWN HOUSE," DERITEND.

The first written record of modern Birmingham is the Domesday survey (1086) which recorded a small manor worth twenty shillings, reflecting the poor-quality agricultural land in the valley of the River Rea and on the adjoining plateau top. Neighbouring manors were worth up to five times more. But the settlement grew, particularly after the de Bermingham family purchased a royal charter for a market in 1166. This initiative, perhaps more than any other, may explain why Birmingham began to grow at the expense of its neighbours, which did not have this legal and economic advantage. By the mid-1300s Aston, once much larger and wealthier, was recorded as merely 'Aston-juxta-Birmingham'. Little trace of the medieval settlement core in the Rea valley survives, although St Martin's church is thought to date from the twelfth century (but little medieval work remains), and the great triangular market place in which it stood survived until the 1960s. The Old Crown pub, in Deritend in the Rea valley, is believed to have originated as a guildhall constructed by the Guild of St John between 1450 and 1500 (Figure 3). The town slowly grew out on to the plateau top and early maps suggest some medieval layout in High Street and New Street.

Although there were some medieval settlements in the area now occupied by Birmingham, the city's main period of growth has been from about 1700, powered by the rapid development of industrialised production, new routes and forms of transportation, and large-scale trade. Some of these villages remain as suburban nuclei, and continuing expansion and administrative boundary changes swallowed up the Royal Borough of Sutton Coldfield in 1974.

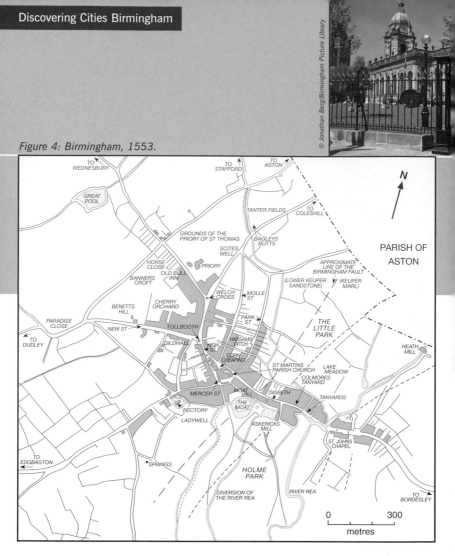

Figure 4: Birmingham, 1553.

Early industrial expansion

By the time of a survey of 1553 the built-up area had expanded north to the site of the Priory (Figure 4) (now Old Square, see Figure 5), partly because the land along the valley side was part of the lord's demesne and was not available for development before the eighteenth century. The early Black Country iron industry was moving southwards, and the first blast furnaces came to Perry Barr in 1538. By 1563 the traveller and topographical writer William Camden wrote that the town was 'swarming with inhabitants, and echoing with the noise of anvils (for here are great numbers of smithes)'. The rivers, although small, provided power for numerous watermills, and these were increasingly used for industrial rather than agricultural purposes. The blade mill in Digbeth

was burned down during the Civil War because it had supplied arms for the Parliamentarians. Birmingham's tradition of Nonconformism began in this period. The town had no borough charter, and so the Act of Parliament banning Nonconformists from coming within 8km of a chartered borough was not applicable.

By the early 1700s the population was about 15,000. A new Baroque-styled parish church was built (later to become the cathedral) and the estates of local wealthy families, such as the New Hall estate immediately north of the new church, began to be developed for middle-class housing.

At this time industry was small-scale, and workshops within or adjoining houses were common. The first

Figure 5: Old Square. Source: Westley, c.1730.

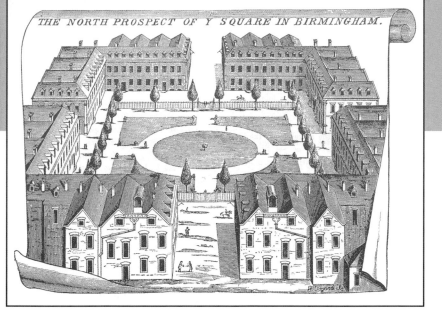

exception to this was Boulton's Soho Manufactory, established in 1761 (Figure 6). Powered by steam (which pumped water for the mill wheel), it produced metal goods, 'toys' and silver plate, and employed over 700 people by 1770, many of whom lived nearby in new industrial housing. It brought complete industrial processes under one roof. (The factory has long since disappeared, but recently Channel 4's 'Time Team' identified and uncovered its foundations.) The traveller Arthur Young described Birmingham in 1791 as 'the first manufacturing town in the world'.

Canals and turnpikes served the ever-growing industries, linking them to national markets. These were vital as the local rivers were not navigable. The canal network grew rapidly from 1772, although water supply on the plateau was a problem. The town was soon well connected by water with the industrial Black Country, which supplied cheap coal. Housing development also

grew, both in density and extent, as a result of industrial prosperity.

However, the medieval core declined as investment and development moved outwards. Hutton, the town's first historian, wrote that 'the space now used as our market was in 1769 completely choked with buildings and filth: the shambles, the round house and the cross nearly filled the area'.

Nineteenth-century industrial boom

The staple industries of guns, jewellery, buttons (which took over from buckle manufacture when shoe fashions changed) and brass continued to grow and remained dominant. As the original wealthy occupants of the new eighteenth-century estates fled the increasing noise and pollution, their houses were converted for industrial production, forming the areas still known as the Jewellery and Gun Quarters, immediately north of the city core

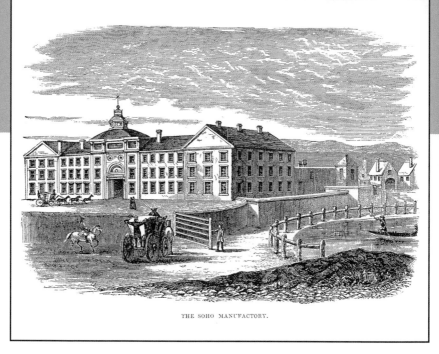

Figure 6: Boulton's Soho manufactory. Source: Dent, c. 1880.

THE SOHO MANUFACTORY.

(see Trail 2, pages 37-40). These industries came here to take advantage of the large properties and the canal. They clustered because of the need for close contact between the numerous specialised small-scale processes involved (about 30 in the case of gun-making).

Financial services were represented by the development of banks, insurance brokers and legal firms. By 1849, of the eight banks operating in the city, six were locally owned, and two (Lloyds and the Midland) continued to the end of the twentieth century.

By the middle of the century Birmingham was at the centre of the country's canal network and, with 53km of navigable canal, it was often said that the city had more canals than Venice. Canal trade continued expanding to its peak in 1898, when 8.5 million tons of cargo were carried.

The railway network also grew, with rival companies competing for routes and space for stations. The first station, the terminus of the London Euston line completed in 1838 at a cost of £5.5 million, still stands impressively in Curzon Street. New Street station bypassed this in 1854, sited in a small valley whose alleyways had been 'packed with brothels and thieves' nests, breeding grounds for typhoid, cholera and crime' (Kellett, 1969). Landownership really determined the position of the network: the Calthorpe and Colmore families objected to the railway, while Sir Thomas Gooch allowed developments on his estate south and east of the core.

The town gained an elected Council in 1838. Prompted by developing public health legislation, by-laws were introduced to regulate new development. One by-law of 1876 effectively banned back-to-back houses. Slum clearance legislation was also used to clear a large

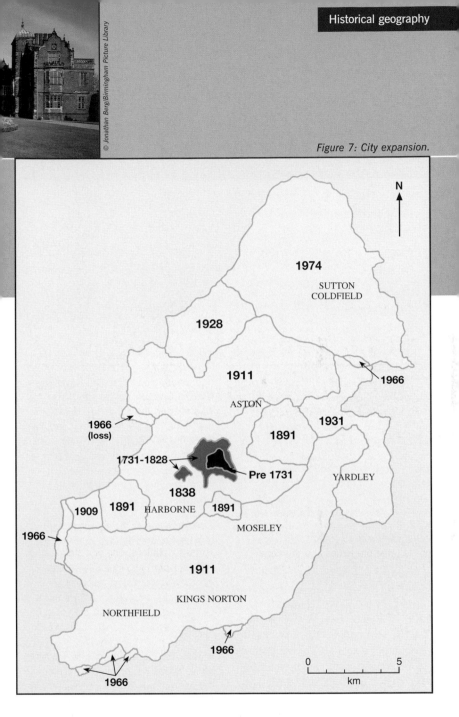

Figure 7: City expansion.

part of the town centre and Corporation Street was built there as a shopping boulevard to rival those of Paris.

During the late nineteenth century the local civic dignitaries (many of whom were Nonconformists) included the Chamberlains, who went on to achieve national political fame. Joseph Chamberlain pioneered improvements in sanitation and urban facilities. City status was conferred in January 1889. Civic pride was demonstrated by increasingly opulent public buildings, including the Town Hall (actually a concert hall, begun in 1834 and modelled on a Roman temple) and the Council House (1874). The Council also acquired the Jacobean Aston Hall, using its grounds for recreation and the house as an early municipal museum which was opened by Queen Victoria. At the

Table 2: Industrial employment in the Birmingham conurbation 1931 and 1948. Source: Kinvig et al. (1951), p.257.

Industry type	1931 (%)	1948 (%)
Commerce	14.0	12.0
Agriculture/mining	2.1	1.5
Metals	39.1	49.2
Public utilities and government	7.2	4.9
Transport	4.9	5.7
Textiles/leather/clothing	4.8	2.6
Professions	2.2	4.4
Miscellaneous	2.3	8.0
Other	23.4	11.7

turn of the century the city's water supply problems were solved with the development of an aqueduct to Wales and a series of dams and reservoirs in the Elan valley.

Expansion began to incorporate neighbouring villages, including Moseley and Harborne. The model village of Bournville was begun at the end of the century on farmland around the Cadbury factory. Yet the unsanitary courtyards and back-to-backs of the inner ring of industrial slum housing persisted, some until well into the next century. The better-constructed housing in the more recently developed fringe districts catered for the wealthier and economically stable working population, not the poorest; indeed Edgbaston was developed by the Calthorpe family as 'the Belgravia of Birmingham'.

Early twentieth-century suburban sprawl

The city continued to grow rapidly in the early part of the twentieth century. It incorporated Quinton in 1909 and, in 1911, there was a threefold expansion with the inclusion of Aston Manor, Handsworth, Erdington, Kings Norton, Northfield and Yardley (Figure 7). The city thus added over 12,140ha

and its population grew to 840,000. A development scheme formulated for Quinton and Harborne was one of the first under the 1909 Housing and Town Planning Act. Bournville rapidly became an international showcase as a 'garden city' development, and was visited by numerous overseas architects and planners.

Civic pride led to the establishment of a new university, supported by the Chamberlains, and originally located in a city-centre college building. An extensive site at Edgbaston was later donated by the Calthorpe family and the new campus, Britain's first, was opened in 1908.

In part, the city's growth was fuelled by new engineering industries, including the Austin (later Rover) car factory at Longbridge from 1906, other vehicle and component manufacturing, and railway carriage construction. The First World War promoted this industrial growth, particularly for armaments.

The growing industrialisation (Table 2), and a realisation that the inner ring contained 200,000 people living in unsanitary housing, led to a major house building drive during the inter-war period. Lloyd George had coined the phrase 'homes fit for heroes' in

Blakesley Hall.

© Jonathan Berg/Birmingham Picture Library

neighbouring Wolverhampton, and Birmingham made full use of it. By 1939 the city had constructed over 50,000 new council houses. Kingstanding had the largest municipal estate (4802 houses) outside London, and overall it re-housed the equivalent of the population of Plymouth. Private housebuilding was also prolific, and new estates of semi-detached houses spread across farmland, particularly to the south and east of the city. Evidence of this process can still be seen in surviving hedgerow trees, estate and field boundaries, and a few pre-urban farmhouses such as Blakesley Hall in Yardley (now a city museum).

Despite the Depression, the city prospered: it led the national employment recovery after 1931. The car industry grew enormously,

although some traditional industries, including jewellery manufacture, declined. A chemical industry developed, with Bakelite being first manufactured here. The newer, extensive factory complexes developed along the Tame valley from Perry Barr to Castle Bromwich (north-east of the city core), and were increasingly dependent on road transport.

By the early twentieth century the city's continued population growth was due more to natural increase than immigration. Net immigration was very low between 1921-31, and there was a net emigration between 1931 and 1951. During the period of inter-war depression, Birmingham remained in a better position than most of the UK's industrial cities.

© Peter J. Larkham

Consolidation, contraction and re-invention

© Peter J. Larkham

Contents

© Peter J. Larkham

Sikh Temple, Graham Street.

© Peter J. Larkham

Post-war replanning

Although Birmingham suffered less bomb damage during the Second World War than many other cities, 5065 houses were destroyed. The Longbridge car factory was only bombed once, and the geographical dispersal of factories across the large city was clearly an advantage. As well as the bomb-damaged houses, there were 110,000 sub-standard houses that needed to be replaced.

Redevelopment areas were identified and compulsorily purchased and major redevelopment work began in the early 1950s. Although the city had for decades resisted large-scale flat development, this was now seen as inevitable and during the 1950s and 1960s the city built over 400 tower blocks. In all, over 81,000 new dwellings were built by the city between 1945 and 1970. Not all were high-rise; there were also some award-winning mixed estates. The modern facilities in the new flats were welcomed at the time, but one key result of this redevelopment was that virtually no residential property remained in the city core, especially in the inner ring. Communities were broken up as new high-rise estates were built at the city's edge, such as Castle Vale and Chelmsley Wood.

Post-war government policies aimed to limit the expansion of larger cities by means of green belts, a network of New and Expanded Towns and other schemes. Birmingham did lose population, particularly to the neighbouring New Town of Redditch and, after some administrative battles, to 'overspill' housing schemes in other neighbouring areas. However, many of these emigrants continued to work in the city, commuting in and out on a daily basis. In 1966, 22% of the city's workers lived beyond its boundaries.

From the 1950s onwards there was significant in-migration to inner city residential areas. Most of the immigrants were Afro-Caribbean, Asian, Indian, or from the Far East, and they tended to congregate in particular parts of the city, forming identifiable enclaves – a feature which was evident from as early as the 1961 Census.

The city centre was also undergoing significant change, in part to replace bomb damage. New shops were built, one block having an innovative tunnel and inner turntable for service vehicle access. An inner ring road, first suggested in 1917, was designed as early as 1943, when the estimated costs were nearly £15 million. The scheme received Ministerial approval in 1957 and was completed in 1971.

Old Bull Ring.

© Jonathan Berg/Birmingham Picture Library

Allied to this was the Bull Ring redevelopment, which cost over £8 million, covered over 9ha, and had over 100 shops, a car-park, offices and bus station. Completed in 1964, it was Europe's first major indoor shopping centre. Adjacent to it was a 25-storey cylindrical office block, the Rotunda, which has become a symbol for the city and is now a Listed Building. A large civic development was also begun, including the largest municipal library in Europe, which opened in 1973. Owing to the oil crisis at that time, part of this development was never completed and the 'scars' can still be seen on the sides of the library.

In 1974 the city's boundaries were changed following a national reorganisation of local government. A new Metropolitan County of the West Midlands was created, which, despite the protests of its residents, added the Royal Borough of Sutton Coldfield to Birmingham (Solihull remained a separate Metropolitan Borough).

Industrial decline and urban dereliction

While Birmingham had been a prosperous city, with unemployment rates below 1% in most years during the 1950s and 1960s, major economic changes from the early 1970s led to contraction in the city's staple industries of heavy engineering and, particularly, car manufacture. Between 1970 and 1983 relative earnings in the region fell from being highest in Britain to almost the lowest of any region. Unemployment rose to 19.4% in 1982 and there were severe social and economic problems in both the inner-ring and outer overspill estates. The industrial geography of the city changed markedly, with long-established companies contracting or closing, and what growth did take place was in the service sector. In 1971, 304,000 people were employed in manufacturing and 277,000 in services; by 1987 this had reversed to 159,000 and 316,000 respectively.

© Jonathan Berg/Birmingham Picture Library

Table 3: Changing employment structure, 1978-2000.
Source: * City Council, Birmingham City Trends 1991;
+ City Council Economic Information Centre.

Activity	% employed			% change 1978-2000
	1978*	1987*	2000+	
Energy and water	1.0	1.0	0.2	-0.8
Metal, mineral, chemical manufacture	5.8	2.5	4.7	-1.1
Metal goods and vehicles	28.4	21.3	5.8	-22.6
Other manufacturing	9.6	7.9	7.2	-2.4
Construction	4.6	4.4	3.4	-1.2
Distribution and catering	15.7	15.6	19.8	+4.1
Transport and communication	5.2	5.4	6.4	+1.2
Finance and business services	7.3	11.7	21.4	+14.1
Other services	22.4	30.1	31.1	+8.7

The oil crisis of 1973 led to widespread recession, and worsened the already visible decline and restructuring of the manufacturing base of both the city and the region. The general economic downturn led to the under- or dis-use of many industrial buildings and their decay and demolition. Municipal development programmes virtually ceased. Between 1971 and 1981 the city's workforce declined by 200,000 to about half a million. Unemployment rates soared, and the inner districts of Deritend, Sparkbrook, Soho and Aston were particularly hard hit.

The industrial economy of the Midlands was over-dependent on one industry, vehicle manufacturing, and this made it vulnerable. Cars are luxury products, and demand fell in the general recession. Labour relations were poor, and strikes frequent. This made the city less attractive to potential investors. Many firms closed down, others consolidated to form larger conglomerates. Table 3 charts this in the changing structure of employment from the late 1970s to 2000.

Another factor in the industrial decline was the unforeseen consequences of the comprehensive redevelopment of the 1950s and 1960s. Small and poor-quality, but cheap, industrial units had

been swept away. Although some purpose-built units had replaced them, these were often unsuited to the requirements of the smaller workshop industries, and too expensive. The 'flatted factory' in the centre of the Jewellery Quarter is a remnant of the 'purpose-built' era.

Social and economic problems persisted into the 1980s, as was noted in the Bishop of Birmingham's report: 'Unemployment levels are high; housing conditions are deteriorating; crime rates are above average; incomes are lower and many are dependent on State welfare benefits. There is often a high incidence of single parent families and of old people living alone. Educational performance and health standards are generally lower than average. These factors are often aggravated by racial prejudice' (O'Brien, 1988, p. 5).

The consequences of these conditions included street riots, especially in the early 1980s.

Regeneration

Recognition of the problems of major industrial decline and a decaying city image led, among other things, to a re-structuring of the city administration, seeking pro-active promotion rather than

National Exhibition Centre.

© NEC Group

reactive control. A 'Development Department' took over the functions of the planning department, and an 'Economic Development Department' was also formed. These were active in promoting the city, attracting major inward investment and facilitating the physical developments that were required by incoming businesses. Early successes were the development of the National Exhibition Centre, on the city fringe, and the expansion of the adjoining airport to form the present Birmingham International Airport. Of course, the success of such ventures was closely related to national, and even global, economic cycles.

Regeneration of the remaining high-density, nineteenth-century residential areas also took place. The city devised an innovative programme whereby streets were 'enveloped', with the outside structure of buildings being refurbished while their residents continue to live in them. This meant that, unlike the 1950s clearance and redevelopment, communities remained intact.

Full use was made of new government funding regimes, including City Challenge and the Single Regeneration Budget, and the Birmingham Heartlands Development Corporation was formed in the badly-affected industrial area to the north-east of the city. Although some of these individual schemes were successful, one problem has been that this funding is competitive and relatively short-lived; some areas succeed at the expense of others, and the long-term effects of this regeneration are yet to be assessed.

The city made some high-profile bids for major national and international events, including the 1992 Olympic Games. Although most of these bids proved unsuccessful, they raised the city's international profile.

In the 1980s a study of open spaces in the central area led to a vision of linkages and the development of more public spaces. This linked the Cathedral with Centenary Square (a large square with much public art, celebrating the centenary of city status) and Brindleyplace, a new 'mixed-use' regeneration area. A concerted urban design study of the entire inner area resulted in the identification of a series of 'quarters'. For most of these a subsequent detailed study has been carried out.

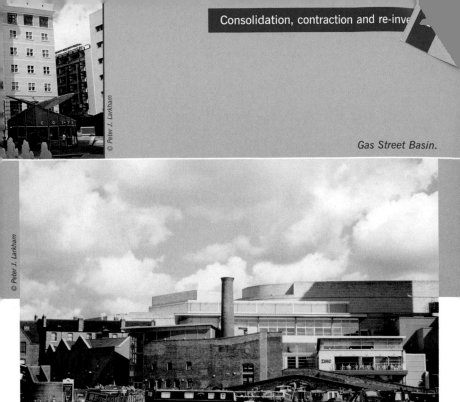

Gas Street Basin.

The 'flagship' redevelopment, of national and international status, was the International Convention Centre, with the world-class acoustics of Symphony Hall. Nearby is the National Indoor Arena, primarily used for indoor athletics and host to the 2003 World Indoor Athletics Championships. Both developments adjoin the central business area. Interestingly, the Convention Centre occupies the site of Bingley Hall, opened in 1850 as the world's first exhibition hall.

A new image for the new century

The planning historian Gordon Cherry wrote that 'Birmingham enjoys an uneven reputation in national esteem. It has never been one of Britain's loved cities; rather it has been derided or shunned' (Cherry, 1994). That may be true historically, but the successes in re-positioning the city's economy, the physical re-structuring of declining areas and the city centre, and an evident cultural renaissance have begun to change that view.

Although the Rover plant has remained in production since its sale by BMW, it is now atypical of the employment pattern in the city. There has been a shift towards the service industries, typified by the attraction of the head office of the Trustee Savings Bank (now Lloyds-TSB) in the 1990s. The city's economic development team aims to establish the city as one of the leading locations for business and commerce in Europe. Business visits and associated tourism are also on the increase, assisted by the International Convention Centre and extension of the National Exhibition Centre. Demand is now exceeding supply, and new construction and refurbishment is under way to provide more hotel accommodation and other facilities for visitors.

Evidence of the city's cultural renaissance includes the internationally famous City of Birmingham Symphony Orchestra and its new Symphony Hall, the extended exhibition space of the Art Gallery and Museum and the re-structuring of the Science Museum in Millennium Point. The city now has

The Water's Edge, Brindleyplace.

© Peter J. Larkham

three universities and a combined student population of some 50,000. It also has the reputation of being the UK's main centre of the balti.

As a post-industrial city, Birmingham has endeavoured over the last two decades to re-position itself in the global economy and has had considerable success thus far. Major urban redevelopment has taken place, and more is programmed. New retail floorspace is countering the decline of city centre shops over the past 15 years, caused by out-of-town shopping centres, particularly the Merry Hill Centre near Dudley. New leisure facilities are of national and international standards, and the International Convention Centre has attracted events such as the 1998 G8 Summit. The Mailbox development is Europe's largest mixed-use refurbishment scheme, more office-to-apartment conversions are under way, and the Brindleyplace redevelopment is recognised as a milestone in urban design (see Trail 3, pages 41-6).

Improvements, including a new urban park, are planned to focus on Millennium Point (a museum, educational and entertainment facility, and the largest Millennium project outside London) on the city's run-down east side.

Of the new central apartments, many have been purchased by companies for business use, although this may change in future. There has been more success in generating inner urban living in edge-of-centre areas such as the Jewellery Quarter, now designated an 'urban village', than in the city core itself.

Changes are not confined to the commercial parts of the city core. A large programme of housing improvement and renewal is ongoing, including refurbishment of tower blocks and the replacement of some by new low-rise housing; and infrastructure improvements are programmed. Yet these changes have not been without their critics. The organisation

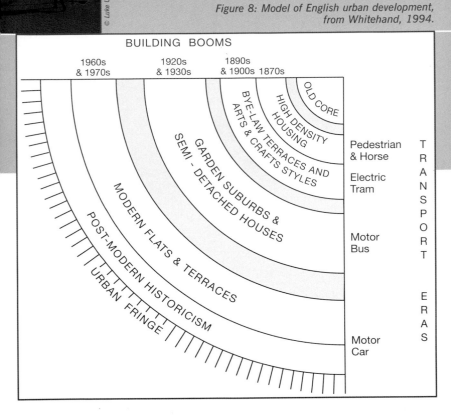

Figure 8: Model of English urban development, from Whitehand, 1994.

© Luke Unsworth/Millennium Point

'Birmingham for People' was set up in the late 1980s to protest against the scale and nature of the first Bull Ring redevelopment proposals, and recent attempts to transfer the city's social housing stock to outside management have been rejected by tenants. But protest has been curiously muted. Even the suggested expansion of Birmingham International Airport (plans include a second international standard runway, terminal and hangars) has created much more outcry in Solihull and Warwickshire than in the city itself.

Thus the city is well-placed to weather the physical, social and economic problems which have beset the city and region. Although a negative image of the city persists in the mass media its remarkable turnaround is evident to the majority of locals and visitors. Given the city's key geographical location in the

centre of the country, at the hub of the national motorway network, it has clear advantages and may well expand further as London-based organisations decentralise and seek new locations. No city is secure in this era of change and competition, but Birmingham's future now has a stronger foundation than many.

Birmingham as a model

Birmingham provides a good context in which to examine a range of geographical concepts relating to how cities are shaped over time, and the traces that remain in the contemporary urban landscape.

Most medieval market towns demonstrate regular patterns in their plot layout, and often in street layouts, because they were planned and laid out

Figure 9: Edwardian fringe belt, from J.W.R. Whitehand and N.J. Moreton.

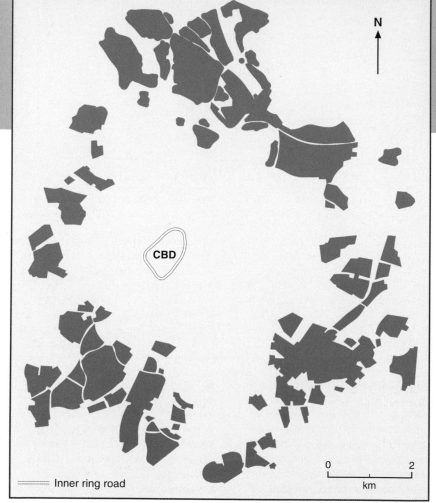

N

CBD

Inner ring road

0   2
km

in one or more phases. Traces of such patterns can be seen in the regular plot widths and lengths shown on eighteenth-century maps of the city, for example on the north side of Digbeth and High Street/Moor Street. Now, however, intensive development has obliterated all traces of these, though the street alignments and names remain: New Street is, of course, a very old street!

As a general rule, the amount, type and location of development from the start of the industrial period to the present is increasingly influenced by large-scale economic fluctuations. In economic booms, land becomes valuable and thus expensive. It tends to be used for high-density, high-profit development such as housing. In a slump, land is cheap, and particular uses that need large sites can be afforded at such times. These include

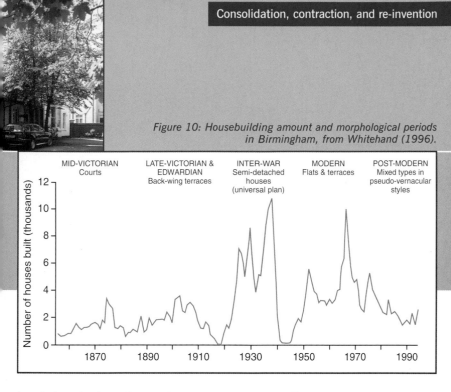

Figure 10: Housebuilding amount and morphological periods in Birmingham, from Whitehand (1996).

hospitals, schools, and recreation facilities. As a town expands outwards, 'pushed' by increasing population and 'pulled' by improving transportation, a 'ring' pattern may develop with higher-density housing followed by a 'fringe belt' of lower-density institutions, then a further phase of housing, and so on (Figure 8). Birmingham retains a very complete, Edwardian, low-density fringe-belt (Figure 9). Earlier fringe belts have often been built up in subsequent boom periods.

The precise location and nature of developments may be determined by 'chance' factors such as a landowner's choices or, more recently, by planning policies. The influence of the major landowning families in determining Birmingham's growth and the location of rail and canal routes has already been mentioned. The Calthorpes developed Edgbaston as a high-class suburb, protecting its quality by means of legal restrictions on land uses (even 'public strawberry-patches' were prohibited).

New developments and the 're-commodification' (conversion to new uses) of older buildings, particularly for retail and office space, change the city's 'centre of gravity', as is well illustrated by Birmingham. The process of development is very uneven, depending as it does on local and national government policies and funding. It is also a dynamic process, with one new project having a knock-on effect on others. For example, a project that is initially successful, such as Brindleyplace, may lose its pre-eminence and vitality to more recent developments elsewhere, e.g. the future Eastside.

Finally, the type and style of buildings changes over time, largely due to changing fashion in architecture and materials and to technological developments. Thus 'morphological periods' can be distinguished in which certain characteristics prevailed and different areas associated with these periods can be identified within a city's landscape (Figure 10).

If morphological periods and the economic fluctuations of development are considered together, a distinctive pattern emerges, as can be seen in Birmingham, particularly in relation to housing.

Small area studies and trails

Contents

© Peter J. Larkham

© Peter J. Lark

© Peter J. Larkham

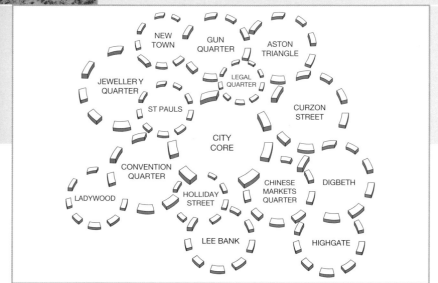

Figure 11: The 'districts' of the city centre. Source: Tibbalds Colbourne Karski Williams (1990) © Birmingham City Council.

NEW TOWN
GUN QUARTER
ASTON TRIANGLE
JEWELLERY QUARTER
LEGAL QUARTER
ST PAULS
CURZON STREET
CITY CORE
CONVENTION QUARTER
CHINESE MARKETS QUARTER
DIGBETH
LADYWOOD
HOLLIDAY STREET
LEE BANK
HIGHGATE

Introduction

In a city of Birmingham's size it is impossible to provide practicable trails to examine all of the trends and developments that have been discussed, so these trails will focus on the city core and two key industrial/residential areas of very different origin and character.

Inevitably, the centre of any sizeable town will, over time, become differentiated in terms of land use and character, leading to the development of distinctive zones. Many of these zones can only be fully understood with reference to the local urban history and the development processes that shaped them. In Birmingham, a number of zones were identified in 1990 as part of an urban design regeneration study (Figure 11).

The city core is delimited by its inner ring road, the 'concrete collar' which is now being broken to encourage people, and economic development, to move outside the tightly-constrained core. The areas into which this growth is spreading are the inner industrial and commercial districts including the markets (to the south), the gun and jewellery quarters (to the north) and some of the inner-ring housing areas, whose industrial slums have been replaced by post-war high-density housing, some of which is already being redeveloped.

There is one further location within the wider city that is worthy of attention – Sutton Park (north of the centre). This adjoins Sutton Coldfield town centre, is readily accessible by public and private transport and is, at 970ha, Europe's largest urban park. It is a managed landscape with a range of ecological communities including heathland, and most of the area has never been cultivated; it contains a Roman road, represents a medieval deer-park and was a gift to the town. It is now a major recreational resource. The management of the semi-natural environments, and the tensions with intensive recreational uses, are of interest. Trails and information are readily available from the park's management (see page 53).

Trail 1.

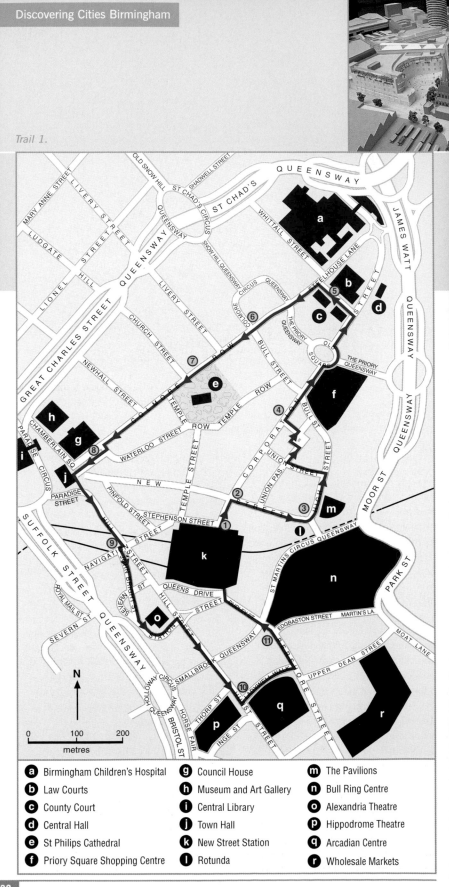

a Birmingham Children's Hospital

b Law Courts

c County Court

d Central Hall

e St Philips Cathedral

f Priory Square Shopping Centre

g Council House

h Museum and Art Gallery

i Central Library

j Town Hall

k New Street Station

l Rotunda

m The Pavilions

n Bull Ring Centre

o Alexandria Theatre

p Hippodrome Theatre

q Arcadian Centre

r Wholesale Markets

Birmingham city centre from Broad Street.

© Jonathan Berg/Birmingham Picture Library

© Jonathan Berg/Birmingham Picture Library

Trail 1: The city core

Distance: 3-4 km

Walking time (without stops):
45 minutes

Disabled access: Yes

Introduction

This trail focuses on the city core and explores the causes and implications of a range of past and ongoing changes. It also breaks out of the 'traditional' core constrained by the inner ring road to touch upon recent retail and leisure developments to the south-east.

As with all city centres, in Birmingham's central area various types of retailing, and other office and civic functions, have tended to cluster together. Originally this minimised the need to travel, facilitating comparison shopping and business in, for example, the municipal office quarter or law quarter. Within Birmingham the city centre has been tightly delineated, since the early 1960s, by the inner ring road. But as circumstances changed in the 1980s-1990s, this became identified as a 'concrete collar', restricting the outward expansion of central business functions and regeneration. Land values dropped very sharply from immediately inside the ring to immediately outside it, so a range

of initiatives was undertaken to break this barrier by downgrading the vehicle road and by promoting developments outside it. The city core's retail centre of gravity has also moved over time, and the current large-scale redevelopment of the Bull Ring – particularly the Selfridges department store – will shift it further to the south-east.

1. The trail begins at the Pallasades shopping centre above New Street station, one of Europe's busiest rail stations and the main public transport gateway to the centre. It was built from 1848 in a small valley of high-density slums, so now the tracks seem to be underground. Walk out of the centre towards New Street. When the new station and shopping centre were built, the exit from the station to the city centre was deliberately routed through the shopping centre. This 'ramp' access, down which flow the great majority of rail passengers, has the largest pedestrian footfall in the city centre, and so property values around here are high. Note the start of Corporation Street; the buildings on the left, c. 1880, have recently been refurbished after proposals to demolish them in favour of a shopping mall were rejected.

New Street.

© Peter J. Larkham

2. Turn right into New Street. New Street itself is a medieval street, built as the town was extending out of the Rea valley onto the plateau. This part of the centre suffered wartime bomb damage and the redevelopment is typical of the post-war period: concrete, plate glass, little architectural detail, and projecting canopies over pavements. The Rotunda, the cylindrical office block on the street corner, was the city's first £1 million office development. It was derided when first built but is now an icon of the city. To its right is the entrance to the new Bull Ring shopping centre. This development deliberately broke the ring road collar on this side of the city. Beyond it lie Digbeth and the original medieval parish church, new market buildings and the Eastside regeneration scheme under way.

3. Turn left and walk up High Street (again evidence of medieval growth). The Pavilions shopping centre obliterated the last trace of medieval burgage plots here. When built in 1987 it was the most expensive, and the only, four-storey, city-centre retail development in the country. How will it be affected by the opening of the Bull Ring? Turn left into Union Street then right through Martineau Square to Corporation Street. Again notice the post-war rebuilding and its recent extensive refurbishment.

4. Corporation Street was constructed following an Act of Parliament of 1876; it involved 18.2ha of slum clearance and cost the city £1.3 million in land acquisition. The then Mayor, Joseph Chamberlain, envisaged 'a great street as broad as a Parisian boulevard' that would make Birmingham 'the retail shop of the Midland Counties of England'. This was an attempt to shift the (high class) retail area. It was unsuccessful because economic conditions meant that the street was built up relatively slowly. Turn right, past Old Square to the Law Courts. Old Square was once the town's finest Georgian square; it is now a bus-only part of the ring road, and has a memorial to the comedian Tony Hancock.

Colmore Row.

5. The Law Courts (Grade 1 Listed, 1887-91) are housed in one of the finest terracotta buildings in the country. Its design influence is Tudor and sixteenth-century Flemish. This is at the hub of a substantial Legal Quarter. Opposite is the Methodist Central Hall (1899-1903), again in terracotta. Its tower is a landmark feature visible along Corporation Street. Terracotta became a characteristic feature of Birmingham's late-Victorian architecture, seen at its best here in the Legal Quarter.

6. Return via Steelhouse Lane, Colmore Circus and Colmore Row. Steelhouse Lane is named after the eighteenth-century Kettle's Steel Houses, which refined imported Swedish iron. Note the unusual post-modern architectural form of the Wesleyan & General building in the centre of Colmore Circus.

7. Colmore Row and much of the area to the right was developed by the Colmore family from the 1750s. Snow Hill station (now rebuilt, and the terminus of the Midland Metro light rail link) and the associated Grand Hotel (1875) are further evidence of the railway influence

in the city. So is the Great Western Arcade (1876), the earliest and best of the city's many shopping arcades. This was built over the Great Western railway cutting. Its original roof and entrance were lost to bomb damage but the 1986 refurbishment is excellent.

Further on the left is St Philip's (1700-20), which became the Cathedral in 1905. Originally designed by Thomas Archer and extended in 1884 by J.A. Chatwin, it is the country's only Baroque cathedral. It has spectacular stained glass by Burne-Jones, made by Morris & Co., typifying the city's involvement with the Arts and Crafts movement. The churchyard railings were reinstated in 2002. Opposite, the Italianate offices of 57-73 Colmore Row (c. 1870), although Listed, were demolished and rebuilt (with the exception of their façades) in the late 1980s. Commercial pressures have triumphed over conservation; but this 'façadism' has happened to about 50% of the buildings in this part of the central conservation area. Further on, the modernist National Westminster bank and the post-modern office next to it show the importance of the

'The River', Victoria Square.

finance sector in the city. Opposite, no. 122 (of 1900) is regarded as being of international importance both in its break with 'historical' styles, and its framed, rather than load-bearing, wall construction.

8. Victoria Square, with its new public art, is a major public space, with the Council House (1874-9) and Town Hall (1832) demonstrating municipal confidence and grandeur. The Town Hall copies a Roman temple, and was originally a concert hall, designed by the inventor of the Hansom cab, Joseph Hansom. The Victorian Post Office, a French Chateau design, was saved by public outcry and converted to the TSB headquarters; but after the merger with Lloyds it is again vacant. The square shows the city's current commitment to public art, although the popular spectacular cascade and statue are locally known as 'the floozy in the jacuzzi'.

9. Walk down Hill Street and note the 'improvements' en route to the southern entertainments quarter; signposted by new lamp standards. John Bright Street was

pedestrianised in the late 1980s but seems now to have lost its vitality to Broad Street; some of its office buildings are now being converted to, or redeveloped as, apartments. There are still some vacant sites here from the 1940s: this could be a 'zone of discard'. The downgrading of the ring road is seen here, where pedestrians originally crossed via subways, in which muggings were common.

10. The long-established Hippodrome Theatre and newer Arcadian Centre have sought to draw pedestrians out of the city core. The Chinese Quarter seems rather a superficial marketing exercise (the city's Chinese population is relatively small). Here, too, is the city's last remaining courtyard slum dwelling, being restored to a museum run by the National Trust.

11. Return to New Street station via Pershore Street and Dudley Street (noting the impact of the original ring road structure on the topography) or through the new Bull Ring to High Street.

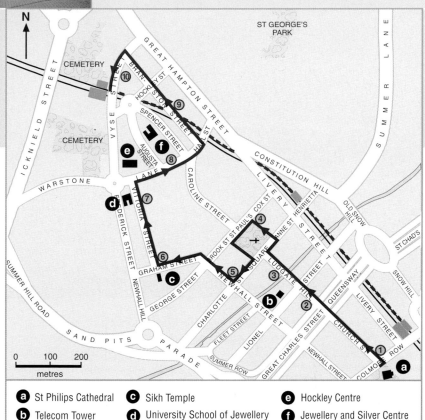

a St Philips Cathedral   **c** Sikh Temple   **e** Hockley Centre

b Telecom Tower   **d** University School of Jewellery   **f** Jewellery and Silver Centre

Trail 2: An industrial history: the Jewellery Quarter

Distance: 2-3km

Walking time (without stops): 40 minutes

Return via public transport: Midland Metro to Snow Hill station

Disabled access: Yes (use pelican crossing across inner ring road just uphill of the pedestrian footbridge)

Introduction

The small-scale metal industries were vital to the city's early industrial growth. Jewellery and guns, in particular, were made by many small-scale specialist processes, by small operations (often individuals). For external economies of scale the trades tended to cluster closely together in specific parts of the town: guns to the north, of which little now remains; jewellery further to the north-east.

Much of the area was originally developed by the city's major land-holding families as larger respectable residential estates, often with a grid street layout. The formal Georgian square of St Paul's, with its central church (1779), typifies this. But fashions change: the wealthy residents moved further out to less-polluted residences, and the houses became industrial workshops. Some were demolished and replaced by factories.

St Paul's, from the Jewellery Quarter.

© Jonathan Berg/Birmingham

By the post-war period, after over a decade of war and economic depression, the jewellery trade was in a bad way. Many of the buildings were in poor repair or derelict. The Council, which was carrying out a major programme of slum clearance and high-rise flat building elsewhere in the city, attempted to rejuvenate the jewellery trade through demolition and construction of a series of multi-storey 'flatted factories'. In the end only one was built, in 1971. It was too large to suit the small-scale nature of the jewellery trade production.

Now, although there is still some workshop production, much of the area seems dominated by jewellery retailing and is marketed as a tourist destination. The Jewellery Quarter is protected by various conservation area designations. More information on the series of artworks set in the pavements of Graham Street, Newhall Hill and Frederick Street is available in the City Council's *Jewellery Quarter Pavement Trails* leaflet, available from the Museum of the Jewellery Quarter on Vyse Street.

This trail starts in the city core, to demonstrate the close historical, physical and developmental links with the Quarter. It is designed as a one-way walk, returning on public transport (the Midland Metro) from the new Jewellery Quarter station to Snow Hill station.

1. The trail begins on Colmore Row at St Philip's Cathedral. The Cathedral is the high-water mark of early urban development, c. 1700-1720. The land to the north-west was owned by the wealthy landowning families and was laid out for high-status residential development but soon became colonised by industry and business. Walk down Church Street. The original buildings, because of their 99-year leases, have all been redeveloped: we see second- and third-generation buildings now. Note the popularity of both French Renaissance and Arts and Crafts styles in the Victorian period, and the various post-war office blocks. The street has a subtle curve; note the vista as you go

Mixed buildings around St Paul's Square.

round this – cathedral behind, church in front.

2. Cross the inner ring road by the footbridge or the pelican crossing just uphill. The ring road marks a major disjunction in property prices and rents; note the high wall of offices behind, and the vacant/derelict sites ahead. In an attempt to promote development on these sites, but also to control its character, the conservation area designation was extended to include these derelict buildings and open car-parks, incongruous though that may seem. Some of the factory buildings ahead have been converted to 'loft apartments'.

3. Continue up Ludgate Hill. You pass over one of the city's many canals: these do not penetrate the city centre because of the topography, so this subtle dip is important. The canals are now extensively used for leisure cruising and as a pedestrian network, although this is not one of the more scenic sections. Note where the 'streetscape improvements' start; this was the edge of the conservation area until its expansion back to the inner ring road. The building uses indicate the area's gentrification.

4. St Paul's Square, a formal Georgian square, is dominated by the church of 1779. Most of the gravestones have been cleared, and the iron rails were removed in the Second World War. Around the square is a mix of original, replica, and new buildings – the latter seeking to restore the enclosed character of the square. There is now a mix of uses including business, leisure and residential.

5. At the Charlotte St/Newhall St junction, note the former world-famous Elkington's electroplating works (1841). This was the city's Science Museum but is now vacant, the museum having moved to Millennium Point. Opposite is the 1878 Assay Office, performing a key function of the Jewellery Quarter. It is the busiest in the world, hallmarking 40,000-70,000 items each working day.

6. Along Newhall St and Graham St are several new apartment buildings designed in 'historic' styles, and the 1844 Congregationalist chapel, which has been re-used as a Sikh temple. Here are the most important surviving factory buildings in the city. That at the corner of Vittoria Street (1839) produced steel pen-

Vyse Street.

nibs: an average worker would cut about 28,000 each day. It is now successfully converted to small business units. The former pen and pencil factory at the corner of Legge Lane and Frederick St is also impressive. But the vacant sites and derelict buildings show the economic problems (and opportunities) in the area.

7. Vittoria Street is the oldest original industrial street in the city. On the left is the UCE School of Jewellery, refurbished and with an award-winning extension. Ahead is the real core of the Jewellery Quarter today.

8. The original dense development of the Georgian and Victorian residential, then industrial, area is interrupted by the post-war clearance: the 'triangle site' ahead. The 'flatted factory' is a relic of the plans to comprehensively redevelop the entire Jewellery Quarter. A more historical monument is the refurbished clock (1903) on the traffic island to the left.

9. On a circuit of the heart of the quarter the mix of jewellery businesses, both manufacturing and, increasingly, retail, is evident. Likewise there is a mix of houses converted to manufacturing/retail use, and new purpose-built retail buildings. Two of the oldest surviving buildings, built as houses in the 1820s, survive as the Reliance Works (Pickering and Mayell, Caroline Street, opposite Spencer Street junction). The name Vyse Street is evidence that this was the Vyse family estate. The Jewellery Quarter Discovery Centre on Vyse Street is a surviving factory/workshop, and provides a good explanation of how the trades worked and, therefore, how this area developed.

10. The only real open space is provided by the cemeteries fronting Vyse Street. The buildings of the Birmingham Mint (also open for tours) can be seen behind. Matthew Boulton's house, Soho House, is open as a museum and education centre, about 1km north off Soho Hill.

Return to Snow Hill by Metro from the new station on Vyse Street. This is itself a good example of regeneration, intended as part of a wider 'light rail' network across the industrial Black Country. This first line links Birmingham and Wolverhampton.

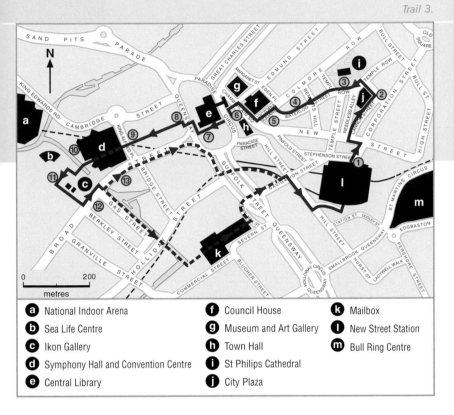

- **a** National Indoor Arena
- **b** Sea Life Centre
- **c** Ikon Gallery
- **d** Symphony Hall and Convention Centre
- **e** Central Library
- **f** Council House
- **g** Museum and Art Gallery
- **h** Town Hall
- **i** St Philips Cathedral
- **j** City Plaza
- **k** Mailbox
- **l** New Street Station
- **m** Bull Ring Centre

Trail 3: Access, regeneration and public space

Distance: 3-4km

Walking time (without stops): 1 hour

Disabled access: Yes (wheelchairs can cross the canal via bridge signposted from inside ICC, or via Broad Street pavement instead of the new canal footbridges; choice of ramp access on return routes)

Introduction

The inner ring road did not solve problems of vehicular congestion within the city centre and the increasing volume of cars caused problems for public transport. Shopping in the city centre became less popular. As the traditional industries declined, the City Council sought to improve the attractiveness of the centre in order to retain existing businesses and to attract more shoppers and tourists. The industrial city was re-inventing itself as a tourist city.

Mechanisms sought to promote the city in this respect included the improvement of the public realm, and major public investment in new business and tourist facilities. First, a meeting of consultants held in Joseph Chamberlain's former house, 'Highbury', and so known as the 'Highbury Initiative', proposed to improve and link a network of public spaces from the city core out towards the west. A series of pedestrianisation schemes, and bus/taxi-only traffic routes, would remove much traffic from the city core. The inner ring road would be downgraded, helping to fuel regeneration to the east, south and west of the core as pedestrian and public transport access became easier.

Convention Place and Centenary Square.

© Jonathan Berg/Birmingham Picture Library

The regeneration initiatives began first in the west. There had long been an exhibition area here (Bingley Hall), the burnt-out remains of which were replaced by a new Symphony Hall and International Convention Centre (ICC). The ICC promoted business tourism; Symphony Hall allowed the promotion of the City of Birmingham Symphony Orchestra, then conducted by Simon Rattle, in this world-class venue. The National Indoor Arena was built just to the north. To the west of the ICC, a large derelict area was redeveloped as Brindleyplace, a pioneering mixed-use regeneration scheme where the city worked closely with the developers in producing a master-plan, and where a number of prominent architects designed innovative buildings.

There have been problems with this approach. While work was undertaken on pedestrianisation schemes, many local traders complained about loss of trade and some left the area. After completion, though, trade has increased significantly. The ICC was part-funded by

European grants, but the City Council had to find its contribution from other budgets: there was considerable debate about the diversion of funds from schools, for example. Brindleyplace was delayed by an economic downturn and liquidation of the developer, and some of the final result was perhaps not as innovative as had been hoped. Nevertheless, the initiative has promoted tremendous additional regeneration along Broad Street, now a significant entertainment quarter, and further out towards the problem post-war redevelopment area of Ladywood.

The trail begins once again at New Street, on the corner access ramp facing Corporation Street.

1. The story of Corporation Street is given in Trail 1, but of note here is the amount of refurbishment of the Victorian buildings at the New Street/Corporation Street junction. The restoration of the head office of the Birmingham and Midland Bank (1869) to become the Waterstones

New Street and Corporation Street.

bookshop is particularly noteworthy; a visit inside will show how many original features have been retained.

The design of the pedestrianisation of New Street, and the amount of traffic on the (supposedly bus-only) Corporation Street, are significant. When first pedestrianised there were complaints from disability groups that the kerbs, paved surface, and positioning of trees and street furniture led to many accidents. Although a much more pleasant environment, often crowded with pedestrians, there is an unexpected vehicle loop between Temple Street and Bennett's Hill that compromises the design.

2. Cannon Street is a narrow back lane, also now pedestrianised. However it is also a service access for the new and refurbished buildings on the right. The refurbishment of the shops on the left is impressive. City Plaza is, perhaps, a less successful scheme owing to its location: i.e. away from major pedestrian routes and less

immediately visible. It took a long time for all of its shop units to be occupied.

3. The Cathedral churchyard is the first in a linked series of public spaces (re)developed following the Highbury Initiative planning exercise in the late 1980s. It has been totally redesigned and its railings, to the original design, reinstated. On sunny days this is a very heavily-used space.

4. Along Waterloo Street note the surrounding buildings. This is a conservation area but under heavy pressure from commercial interests. Many buildings have suffered 'façadism' (modern redevelopment behind a retained historic façade). Bennett's Hill (laid out 1827) was named after the family who farmed here.

5. Victoria Square is the second public space. There was once a church on the corner of New Street/Colmore Row, with a busy road running around it. After the Second World

Convention Place, towards the ICC.

© Peter J. Larkham

War the area was grassed, and again heavily used by the public on fine days. In the 1990s the area was pedestrianised and redesigned, after public consultation, with commissioned public art to create a better setting for the Town Hall and Council building. (However, the public wanted more grass for sitting out!)

6. The next in the chain of spaces is Chamberlain Square. It was laid out in this fashion in the 1960s after demolition of the previous Library and Mason College. The stepped circle is very popular for meetings and events. The fountain (1880) commemorates Joseph Chamberlain's contribution to municipal life (although he had not yet become an MP). The Museum and Art Gallery has a spectacular Victorian iron and glass exhibition hall, and a good collection of Pre-Raphaelite art.

7. The Central Library is one of Europe's largest, but is part of a substantial development that was halted by the 1973 oil crisis (this is particularly evident on the far side)

and was famously referred to by Prince Charles as appearing to be a place for incinerating books rather than keeping them. Recent plans suggest the £900 million redevelopment of this area and removal of the library to the Eastside regeneration area. Originally the space under the library was open; it was roofed and various food retail units developed in the early 1990s. There was much debate about maintaining 24-hour access versus the operators' concern for security: an example of the attempted privatisation of public space.

8. The new bridge is an example of the improvement of pedestrian access along this network of spaces. At considerable cost, this involved lowering the entire inner ring road at this site and constructing this new wide pedestrian bridge, improving access to the ICC, Symphony Hall and other facilities.

9. There was open space here from the early years after the First World War, when the Hall of Memory was built. There has long been a desire for a Civic Quarter here, and originally all

© Peter J. Larkham

'Forward', Centenary Square.

© Peter J. Larkham

buildings were to be classically-styled and of white Portland stone. Few buildings of this type were actually built. Baskerville House (to the right) was begun in 1936 but only part-built owing to the war. Until recently it housed Council departments, and conversion for office use is now planned. Opposite 'Arena Central' is planned, a £400 million mixed-use development, originally designed to be the country's tallest building. The Square, with its public art, was laid out in 1989 to commemorate the centenary of city status. The paving, and Raymond Mason's interpretation of the city's industrial history and its motto 'Forward', are noteworthy.

10. The International Convention Centre and Symphony Hall were two parts of a major redevelopment on the site of Bingley Hall, before that the house of Sampson Lloyd, a founder of Lloyd's bank. They are separated by a covered mall. This was designed and oriented as part of the planned pedestrian axis. The West Coast Main Line railway runs underneath Symphony Hall, causing significant problems of noise and vibration which have been overcome by innovative design. The ICC is directly linked to the Hyatt Regency Hotel across Broad Street by a private footbridge, a concept familiar in some US cities.

11. Cross the canal to Brindleyplace (wheelchair access signposted within the ICC mall). The first-phase retail and leisure units facing the canal have a waterfront/industrial design idiom. The main part of this major regeneration scheme completed the public space route with a wholly new square and its small café. All of the buildings are distinctive, most being designed by well-known architects (e.g. Piers Gough, the café; Lord Rogers, the Sea Life Centre). To the left is a Japanese-inspired square outside the Ikon Gallery (a former school, restored as an art gallery as part of the redevelopment). Most of

The Mailbox.

the surrounding buildings were offices, but many have other ground-floor functions. To the right, facing the canal, is a development of apartments using Dutch canal-side designs.

12. On Broad Street notice how the regeneration has spread along the street, with the conversion of many shops (and a church) to pubs, bars and clubs. At night this area is thriving – the presence of three universities in the city partly explains its success! To the right is Gas Street canal basin, accessed along Gas Street (but wheelchair access is past the Hyatt Regency Hotel, down Bridge Street, again because of a traditional-style canal footbridge; or by lift from the Brindleyplace footbridge down to towpath level). This historic basin is where the projects of two canal companies met. On the plateau, supplying water for the canals was problematic, so there is a 'stop lock' where boats would be charged a fee

to move from one canal to the other. New buildings line the east waterfront, with some original buildings remaining on the west side. The basin is now very popular with touring boats. Canal trips can be arranged.

13. Return to New Street along the canal towpath, across a ramped bridge and through the Mailbox development; or via the footbridge over the inner ring road (which has ramped access; alternatively use underpass in front of the Mailbox). Note the refurbishment of the former Royal Mail sorting office as the 'Mailbox', a mixed-use development which has a Harvey Nichols branch amongst other high-quality shops, and extremely expensive apartments. Other neighbouring buildings are also being converted into apartments. Attempts are being made to link the Mailbox with the city centre by public art and improvements along Navigation Street.

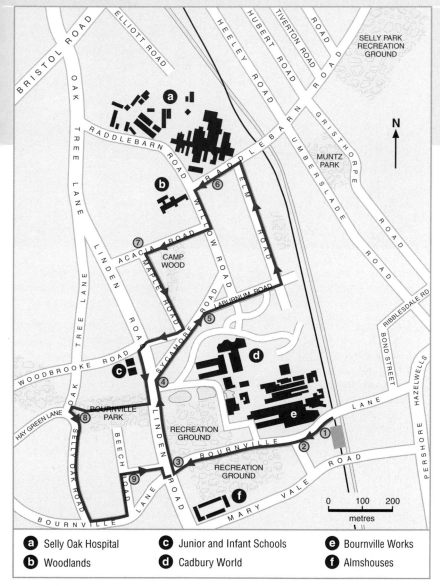

a Selly Oak Hospital   **c** Junior and Infant Schools   **e** Bournville Works

b Woodlands   **d** Cadbury World   **f** Almshouses

Trail 4: The classic garden suburb: Bournville

Distance: 3-4 km

Walking time (without stops):
45 minutes

Disabled access: Yes

Introduction

Bournville is one of the group of classic late-Victorian 'model villages', along with Port Sunlight, Saltaire and others. They were built by industrialists as showpieces of contemporary residential architecture and planning. Bournville has its origins in 1879 when the Cadburys moved their chocolate factory

Bournville.

from the city centre to a farmland site 6.5km to the south-west. It had good rail and canal access, and provided cleaner, more hygienic surroundings for food manufacture.

Although some houses were built next to the factory in 1879 for key workers, the 'village' itself began in the mid-1890s when George Cadbury purchased an adjoining 49ha site, and appointed Alexander Harvey as his architect. His aim, according to the Deed establishing Bournville Village Trust in 1900 to manage the estate, was 'to be the amelioration of the condition of the working-class and labouring population in and around Birmingham, and elsewhere in Great Britain, by the provision of improved dwellings, with gardens and open spaces to be enjoyed therewith'.

The village was not purely for workers in Cadbury's factory (unlike Lord Lever's Port Sunlight) and, as the city grew outwards, has always been an integral part of the city rather than an isolated suburb. The Trust has always actively managed the original 'village' and its later stages of growth, to the north-west of Bristol Road. The village was host to many visits by overseas planners and

architects, and was a very influential development at the time when the garden city concept was growing in popularity.

More recently there has been some gentrification, particularly as the 'right to buy' policy took properties out of the Trust's ownership. The growth of the nearby university and hospital made it a desirable location for staff. Nevertheless the sense of community remains strong, although that key English village feature – the pub – is missing (the Cadburys were Quakers). The village is now a conservation area, and Cadbury World (part of the factory) a major tourist destination.

The trail begins at Bournville railway station on Bournville Lane (there are frequent trains from New Street station in the city centre).

1. First, it is worth exploring under the rail/canal bridge to see the typical late-nineteenth century industrial terraced housing on Bournville Lane and the surrounding cul-de-sacs. These should be compared with the pattern of development on the Bournville estate, built at much the same period.

The carillon, Bournville Junior School.

2. There is an information plaque about the factory nearly opposite the station. Further up Bournville Lane, the very first semi-detached houses, built for foremen etc, were approximately where the Baths are. The architectural historian Pevsner calls the Baths (1904) 'the most impressive architectural extravaganza of the whole estate'. There are extensive recreation grounds to both left and right, and a group of Tudor-style almshouses fronting on to Linden Road.

3. Past the factory and Cadbury World is the village green. Here are the public buildings and a row of shops. Although sites were allocated, some were not built until the 1920s (the church, for example, is of 1925). The Junior Schools, fronting Linden Road, have a most unusual feature in England, a carillon (set of bells) which was added in 1934: rumour has it after Cadbury visited Belgium and liked the carillon tradition there.

4. Note the arcadian nature of the road names, e.g. Sycamore Road, Maple Road. Both of the timber-framed

buildings here were originally sited elsewhere in the city, purchased in the early 1900s in derelict state, dismantled and brought here, and re-erected. Both have fourteenth-century origins, and add to the traditional village appearance of the Green. They are now used as a small museum.

5. Along Sycamore Road and Laburnum Road note the size and variation of houses. When built, emphasis was placed on the gardens: unusually, they were fenced and laid out before the houses were occupied. There are evident problems in trying to accommodate cars in an urban landscape not designed for them. There are some rare survivals here of the prefabricated garages sold with their vehicles by large car manufacturers such as Austin and Morris, but the Trust is trying to resist conversion of gardens to parking spaces.

6. In Elm Road, Raddlebarn Road, and Willow Road the nature and size of houses has changed. Note the standardised glass porches fitted to

Housing at Bournville.

many houses in the 1950s/60s by the Trust. A short diversion along Raddlebarn Road reveals the main block of the hospital, formerly the district workhouse.

7. On Acacia Road there are some bungalows for the elderly. On Maple Road there are some very large houses, although some are disguised and are, in fact, semi-detached. On the estate this is not uncommon; there are some semi-detached blocks that are actually four separate flats: look for multiple front doors. Note the nursery, now a garden centre: this is an original feature of the village, providing (in particular) fruit and vegetable plants for the substantial gardens. Compare with the standard terraces seen earlier.

8. Over Linden Road, note the valley parkway along Griffin's Brook. Oak Tree Lane pre-dates the village layout; there are some more standard Victorian terraces around the Hay Green Lane junction. Along Selly Oak Road there are more bungalows for the elderly.

9. Along Bournville Lane and Beech Road look particularly at the size and type of houses. Significantly larger and later than the Elm Road/Willow Road area, they often contain elements of Birmingham Arts and Crafts architecture, and form what would now be seen as a typical middle-class arcadian suburb. Return along Bournville Lane to the station.

Bibliography and further information

Atkins, P. (1989) 'The architecture of Bournville 1879-1914', in Tilson, B. (ed) *Made in Birmingham: Design and industry 1889-1989.* Studley: Brewin, pp. 35-48.

Birmingham City Council (1993) *Unitary Development Plan.* Birmingham: City Council. (Under review: revised draft published in 2001)

Borg, N. (1973) 'Birmingham' in Holliday, J. (ed) *City Centre Redevelopment.* London: Charles Knight, pp. 30-77.

Bournville Village Trust (1955) *Bournville Village Trust 1900-1955.* Birmingham: Bournville Village Trust.

Briggs, A. (1952) *History of Birmingham, Vol. 2.* Oxford: Oxford University Press.

Bryson, J.R. and Lowe, P.A. (1996) 'Bournville: A hundred years of social housing in a model village' in Gerrard, A.J. and Slater, T.R. (eds) *Managing a Conurbation: Birmingham and its region.* Studley: Brewin, pp. 262-75.

Chapman, D., Harridge, C., Harrison, J., Harrison, G. and Stokes, B. (eds) (2000) *Region and Renaissance: Reflections on planning and development in the West Midlands, 1950-2000.* Studley: Brewin.

Cherry, G.E. (1994) *Birmingham: A study in geography, history and planning.* Chichester: Wiley.

Chinn, C. (1991) *Homes for People: 100 years of council housing in Birmingham.* Birmingham: Birmingham Books.

Chinn, C. (1993) *Keeping the City Alive: 21 years of urban renewal in Birmingham 1972-93.* Birmingham: City Council.

Chinn, C. (ed) (2003) *Birmingham: Bibliography of a city.* Birmingham: Birmingham University Press.

Development Department, Birmingham City Council (1989) *Developing Birmingham 1889-1989: 100 years of city planning.* Birmingham: City Council.

Ember, M. and Ember, C. (eds) (2002) *Encyclopedia of Urban Cultures.* Danbury, CT: Grolier.

Gill, C. (1952) *History of Birmingham, Vol. 1.* Oxford: Oxford University Press.

Gledhill, A. (1988) *Birmingham's Jewellery Quarter.* Studley: Brewin.

Harrison, M. (1999) *Bournville: Model village to garden suburb.* Chichester: Phillimore.

Hillman, J. (1994) *The Bournville Hallmark: Housing people for 100 years.* Studley: Brewin.

Johnson, R. (2002) 'Britain's Boom town', Sunday Times Magazine, 28 July.

Kellett, J.R. (1969) *Railways and Victorian Cities.* London: Routledge and Kegan Paul.

Kinvig, R.H., Smith, J.G. and Wise, M.J. (eds) (1951) *Birmingham and its Regional Setting.* Birmingham: British Association for the Advancement of Science.

Latham, I. and Swenarton, M. (eds) (1999) *Brindleyplace: A model for urban regeneration.* London: Right Angle.

Noszlopy, G. (1997) *Public Sculpture of Birmingham including Sutton Coldfield.* Liverpool: Liverpool University Press.

O'Brien, R. (1988) *Faith in the City of Birmingham.* Exeter: Paternoster Press.

Paris, C. and Blackaby, B. (1979) *Not Much Improvement: Urban renewal policy in Birmingham.* London: Heinemann.

Pevsner, N. and Wedgewood, A. (1966) *The Buildings of England: Warwickshire.* London: Penguin, pp. 98-214.

Slater, T.R. (2002) *Edgbaston.* Chichester: Phillimore.

Slater, T.R. and Larkham, P.J. (1996) 'Whose heritage? Conserving historical townscapes in Birmingham' in Gerrard, A.J. and Slater, T.R. (eds) *Managing a Conurbation: Birmingham and its region.* Studley: Brewin, pp. 241-61.

Smith, B.M.D. (1989) 'The Birmingham Jewellery Quarter: A civic problem that has become an opportunity in the 1980s' in Tilson, B. (ed) *Made in Birmingham: Design and industry 1889-1989.* Studley: Brewin, pp. 96-112.

Spencer, K., Taylor, A., Smith, B.M.D., Mawson, J., Flynn, N. and Batley, R. (1986) *Crisis in the Industrial Heartland: A study of the West Midlands.* Oxford: Clarendon Press.

Stephens, W.B. (ed) (1964) *Victoria County History of Warwick. Vol VII: The city of Birmingham.* Oxford: Oxford University Press.

Sutcliffe, A. (1986) 'The "Midland Metropolis": Birmingham 1890-1980' in Gordon, G. (ed) *Regional Cities in the UK 1890-1980.* London: Harper and Row, pp. 25-40.

Sutcliffe, A.R and Smith, R. (1974) *History of Birmingham, Vol. 3.* Oxford: Oxford university Press.

Tibbalds Colbourne Karski Williams (1990) *Birmingham Urban Design Strategy.* Birmingham: City Council.

Upton, C. (1993) *A History of Birmingham.* Chichester: Phillimore.

Whitehand, J.W.R. (1994) 'Development cycles and urban landscapes', *Geography,* 79, 1, pp. 3-17.

Whitehand, J.W.R. (1996) 'Making sense of Birmingham's Townscapes', in Gerrard, A.J. and Slater, T.R. (eds) *Managing a Conurbation: Birmingham and its region.* Studley: Brewin, pp. 226-40.

© Jonathan Berg/Birmingham Picture Library

Tourist information centres
2 City Arcade, Birmingham B2 4TX.
Tel: 0121 202 5000
There is also a small information desk in
the ICC, Broad Street, Birmingham B1 2EA

Sutton Park Visitor Centre
Nr Town Gate, Sutton Coldfield
B74 2YT. Tel: 0121 355 6370

Local Studies Library
Birmingham City Archives and Local
Studies sections, Central Library,
Chamberlain Square, Birmingham
B3 3HQ.

Maps
Geographer's A-Z Map Company *A-Z
Street Atlas Birmingham* (1:18,103)

Ordnance Survey *Landranger 139:
Birmingham* (1:50,000)

Ordnance Survey large-scale maps of
c. 1890-1910 are reprinted by Alan
Godfrey Maps, Consett.

Websites
BBC Midlands
www.bbc.co.uk/birmingham

beinbirmingham
www.birmingham.org.uk

Birmingham City Council
www.birmingham.gov.uk

Birmingham International Airport
www.bhx.co.uk

Birmingham Museums & Art Gallery
www.bmag.org.uk

Birmingham Picture Library
www.bplphoto.co.uk

Birmingham Post and Mail
icbirmingham.icnetwork.co.uk

Bull Ring redevelopment
www.bullring.co.uk

European Capital of Culture bid
www.beinbirmingham2008.net

History and heritage
www.birminghamheritage.org.uk

History of the city, by William Dargue
www.bgfl.org/bgfl/activities/intranet/ks4/
history/birmingham

How it was in central Birmingham
c. 1850-1914, by Sarah Hinksman
www.cs.aston.ac.uk/oldbrum

Images and life
www.millennibrum.org

Tourist guide
www.s-h-systems.co.uk/tourism/
birmingham
www.birminghamuk.com

Virtual Brum
www.virtualbrum.co.uk

Photo credits

The GA would like to thank the following for their help with photographs for this book:

- Jonathan Berg, Birmingham Picture Library
- Luke Unsworth, Millennium Point
- MG Rover
- NEC Group
- Peter J. Larkham
- Sutton Coldfield local studies library
- University of Birmingham Field Archaeology Unit